Festivals of the World

ISRAEL

Gareth Stevens Publishing
MILWAUKEE

Written by
DON FOY

Edited by
SUSAN MCKAY

Designed by
JAILANI BASARI

First published in North America in 1997 by
Gareth Stevens Publishing
1555 North RiverCenter Drive, Suite 201
Milwaukee, Wisconsin 53212 USA

For a free color catalog describing Gareth
Stevens' list of high-quality books and
multimedia programs, call
1-800-542-2595 (USA)
or 1-800-461-9120 (Canada).
Gareth Stevens Publishing's Fax: (414) 225-0377
See our catalog, too, On the World Wide
Web: http://gsinc.com

Printed in Singapore

© **TIMES EDITIONS PTE LTD 1997**
Originated and designed by
Times Books International
an imprint of Times Editions Pte Ltd
Times Centre, 1 New Industrial Road
Singapore 536196

Library of Congress Cataloging-in-Publication Data
Foy, Don.
    Israel / by Don Foy.
    p. cm. — (Festivals of the world)
Includes bibliographical references and index.
Summary: Describes how the culture of Israel is
reflected in its many festivals, including Pesach,
Sukkot, and Hanukkah.
    ISBN 0-8368-1684-6 (lib. bdg.)
1. Fasts and feasts—Judaism—Juvenile literature.
2 Festivals—Israel—Juvenile literature. [1. Fasts
and feasts—Judaism. 2. Festivals—Israel. 3.
Israel—Social life and customs.] I. Series
    BM690.F694 1997
296.4'3'095694—dc20   96-31953

1 2 3 4 5 6 7 8 9 99 99 98 97

CONTENTS

It's Festival Time . . .

Most Israeli festivals are religious. This means that the festivals are a celebration of the Jewish faith. In Israel, festivals usually include a story to remind people why they are celebrating. Many of the stories come from the Bible and tell of things that happened long ago. Some of the festivals may seem very serious, but others are lively, with the whole family and community participating. So why don't you come along, too? It's festival time in Israel . . .

WHERE'S ISRAEL?

I srael is part of the region known as the Middle East, which lies between North Africa and Asia. It is a small country, only slightly larger than the state of New Jersey. Israel only became a country in 1948, but the history of the area is very old. People have lived there for at least 100,000 years. Many of the events in the Bible took place in the land we now call Israel. The capital of Israel is Jerusalem. Jerusalem is a holy city for Christians, Muslims, and Jews.

Who are the Israelis?

Nearly all of the people living in Israel are Jewish. Many of them have come to Israel from different places around the world. Any Jewish person can become a citizen of Israel once they arrive in the country. Recently, people have come to Israel from countries that used to be part of the Soviet Union, such as Russia and Ukraine. During the famine in Ethiopia in the 1980s, thousands of Jewish people were helped by the Israeli government to settle in Israel. Even though these people have different backgrounds, they are united by their Jewish faith.

This young Israeli boy is holding the **Torah**, the Jewish holy book.

Most of the other people living in Israel are Arabs, and they practice a different religion, called Islam. Throughout the rest of the Middle East, Islam is the most common religion but in Israel, Muslims are a **minority**. A small number of Christians also live in Israel. Christianity was introduced to this part of the world hundreds and hundreds of years ago.

The rock over which The Temple of the Dome was built is sacred to Jews and Muslims. This is where Abraham went to sacrifice his son Isaac. It is also where Muhammad is said to have ascended to heaven.

ISRAEL

LEBANON

MEDITERRANEAN SEA

Hula Lake

SYRIA

Hills of Galilee

Haifa

Nazareth

Mount Carmel

Sea of Galilee

GOLAN HEIGHTS

Kishon

Hadera

Tel Aviv-Jaffa

Temple Mount

WEST BANK

JERUSALEM

Jericho

Mount Zion

Gaza

Bethlehem

Hebron

GAZA STRIP

Besor

Dead Sea

Negev Desert

JORDAN

EGYPT

N

Elat

Gulf of Aqaba

WHEN'S THE CELEBRATION?

I n biblical times, people used a calendar based on the moon, called the
lunar calendar. This is different from the calendar we use, which is
based on the sun and is called the solar or Gregorian calendar.
Although the Gregorian calendar is used for everyday life in Israel,
important dates, such as holidays and festivals, are decided using the
lunar calendar. This means that the dates of holidays and festivals in
Israel change each year.

SPRING
- **TU BI-SHEVAT** (New Year of the Trees) ● **PESACH** (Passover)
- **GOOD FRIDAY**—In Jerusalem, church bells ring, calling people
  to remember Jesus.
- **EASTER**—Hundreds of people walk the route Jesus walked the
  day he was crucified.
- **PURIM** (Feast of Esther)
- **MEMORIAL DAY**
- **INDEPENDENCE DAY**

SUMMER
- **SHAVUOT**—People decorate the
  synagogue with green shoots and fruits
  to celebrate the grain harvest.

Wave your flag for Simhat Torah on page 15.

AUTUMN

- **ROSH HOSHANAH** (Jewish New Year)—Jewish families gather for a feast on the first night. On the second night, new fruits are eaten for the first time and a special blessing is said.
- **YOM KIPPUR** (Day of Atonement)—Jews fast on this day to pay the penalty for their sins the year before.
- **SUKKOT** ✪ **SHEMINI ATZERET**
- **SIMHAT TORAH** (Rejoicing of the Law)

WINTER

- **HANUKKAH** (Festival of Lights)
- **HOLOCAUST MEMORIAL DAY**
- **CHRISTMAS**

MUSLIM HOLIDAYS

- **MAWLID EL-NABI** (Prophet Muhammad's Birthday)
- **ID-AL-FITR** (Feast of Breaking the Fast)—Muslims have a three-day feast to break the month-long fast of Ramadan. People dye their hands orange as a symbol of good luck.
- **ID-AL-ADHA** (Feast of the Sacrifice)—Muslims honor Ishmael, the father of the Arab people, by sacrificing and roasting a sheep. After the feast, any extra food is given to the poor.

Keep on marching to page 22 for Independence Day.

PESACH

Pesach (Passover in English) is the oldest festival in Israel. It was first celebrated more than 3,000 years ago! In every Jewish household the father tells the story of Pesach, while the family eats a special meal called *Seder* [SAY-dur]. Passover lasts for eight days.

Listen to a story . . .

Many years ago the Hebrews (that's what Jews were called) moved to Egypt to look for better land and food. The Hebrews were a small group when they arrived in Egypt, but they were known as hard workers and they were admired for their wisdom. In time, the leader of Egypt, called the Pharaoh, became worried that the clever Hebrews would turn against him, so he made them slaves. The Jewish people were forced to make bricks to build Egyptian cities. They cried out to God for help, and finally their prayers were answered. Terrible things started to happen to the Egyptians. Boils broke out on their skin, and thousands of frogs covered the land. The Egyptians were so caught up with their problems that they let the Jews escape.

The story of the Jews' escape from Egypt is called the **Haggadah**. On the first day of Pesach, parents tell their children the story so they will feel what the slaves felt and appreciate their freedom.

The great escape

When the Jews were escaping from Egypt, they didn't have much time. They had to pack up all their things in a hurry. But what about food? If you have ever made bread, you know that it takes a long time for the bread to rise and get fluffy. If the Jews had waited for the bread, they might have been caught by the Egyptians. So instead they packed bread without any yeast, so it was flat and easy to carry. The bread is called *matzah* [ma-TZA], and it is what all Jews eat during Pesach. In fact, bakeries aren't even open during Pesach because no one is allowed to eat leavened bread (bread with yeast) for the eight days of Passover.

The Pharaoh sent his army after the escaping Jews. The Bible says that when the Jews reached the Red Sea, God parted it for them to walk through. But when the Egyptians tried to go through, the sea came together again and drowned them all.

These two Israeli children are eating matzah, the flat, crispy bread that all Jews eat at Passover.

Burning the hametz

The week before Pesach, the whole house is cleaned from top to bottom. This is to make sure that there is no yeast in the house. Sometimes little pieces of **hametz** [ha-METZ], as yeast is called in Hebrew, are left around the house, and it's the children's job to find them. The children go through the whole house with a candle and a feather to be sure it is clean. If they find any yeast, it has to be burned. The next day the family makes a big fire outside. They throw in all the yeast and burn it all away.

A family of Jews gathers in the courtyard to burn the last of the hametz.

The Seder

The word *Seder* means "order." The food for the Seder meal is laid out in a special order to remind people of the escape from Egypt. This is a time for sharing. Many families invite students away from home or poor people to join them for Seder. After the leader breaks the bread, he says, "Let all who are hungry come and share this meal." Some people leave the door open during Seder so anyone who is hungry can come in and eat.

This is a Seder plate. On the plate there is a place for each one of the special foods that are eaten during the Seder to remind Jews of their struggle against slavery. There is also matzah, wine, and a bowl of salt water.

Hunting for the afikoman

At the beginning of the meal, the leader of the Seder breaks one piece of matzah in two. Half is left on the table, and the other half, called the *afikoman* [a-fi-ko-MAN], is hidden. After the story of Pesach has been told, all the children go afikoman-hunting. The afikoman is very important because the Seder can't be finished until everyone eats a piece of it. And the child who finds it is very lucky because the Seder leader has to pay ransom for the bread!

Did you know?

The Jewish bible, the Torah, says that a father must tell his children the story of Pesach on the eve of the festival. Today, many fathers also tell stories of more recent Jewish struggles against slavery. On Seder night, everyone leans on big, comfortable cushions. This is because slaves used to sit on hard stools without cushions. Today Jews lean on the pillows to show that they are free.

A family sits down to enjoy their Seder. Each one of the special foods is on the plate with the matzah at the front.

SUKKOT

Sukkot is one of Israel's harvest festivals. It takes place in the autumn. It's a time to give thanks for the food that has grown through the summer months. Today, the harvest is not as important as it was in ancient times, but Sukkot is still one of the most important festivals in Israel and for Jews everywhere.

This little girl is wearing a flower wreath to celebrate the harvest.

Listen to a story . . .

As with all Jewish celebrations, there is a story behind Sukkot. After escaping from slavery in Egypt, the Jewish people wandered for 40 years in the desert. To protect themselves from the harsh weather, they built huts to live in. These huts were called *sukkot* [su-KOT] (just one is called a **sukkah**), which is where the festival got its name. According to the Jewish holy book, every family must build a sukkah during the festival. If you are in Israel during Sukkot, you will see plenty of sukkot decorated with fruits and vegetables to celebrate the harvest. During Sukkot, people eat their meals in the sukkah, and some people even sleep there!

According to the Torah, the sukkah must be no higher than 30 feet (9 m), must have at least three walls, and the roof must be made of leaves and straw. There must be enough open space in the roof for the stars to be seen.

Opposite: These people are putting on a Sukkot play. They are dressed the way the Hebrews would have been after they escaped into the desert.

Lulav and etrog

The *lulav* [lu-LAV] and the *etrog* [et-ROG] are symbols of the harvest. The etrog is a type of fruit, much like a lemon, from a tree called the citron. The lulav is made up of the branches of three different trees—the palm tree, the willow tree, and the myrtle tree. The branches are tied together and carried throughout the week-long Sukkot celebrations.

The seventh day of the festival is called Hoshana Rabbah. On this day, people celebrate by walking seven times around the synagogue, carrying the branches and fruit. As they parade around, they shout "Hoshana"—"God help us"—and this is why the day is called Hoshana Rabbah, which means Great Hoshana.

Shemini Atzeret

Sukkot lasts for seven days, but because another holiday falls right after it, Jews actually celebrate for eight days. The eighth day of Sukkot is called Atzeret or Shemini Atzeret, which means the "Eighth day of Assembly." Shemini Atzeret is the day when Israelis say a prayer for rain, called *geshem* [GE-shem]. Because Sukkot celebrates the harvest, people think a lot about the rain that helps the crops grow. In Israel, where the land is very dry, rain is a symbol of God's mercy. For the people who work and live on farms, the Sukkot festival is still a celebration of the harvest and the rain. In the cities, because people do not farm the land, the harvest is remembered and celebrated with the sukkah and the lulav and etrog. In this way, Jews, not only in Israel but all over the world, are linked together by their festivities and their religion.

This man is reading from the Torah while he walks around the synagogue on Hoshana Rabbah.

Simhat Torah

Simhat Torah is actually the ninth day of Sukkot, but in Israel it is combined with Shemini Atzeret. Simhat Torah is a celebration of the Torah. Throughout the year, a part of the Torah is read on every Monday, Thursday, and each Sabbath. Jews begin reading the Torah in the synagogue on Simhat Torah and finish on the same day the following year.

Everybody sings and dances in the streets during a Hakkafot parade.

Simhat Torah is the happiest holiday of all. On the eve of Simhat Torah, Jews sing and dance in the synagogues. They carry the Torah scrolls as they celebrate. The festivities in the synagogues often spill out into the streets. These street celebrations are called Hakkafot parades. The Torah scrolls are carried at the front of the parade. The children follow, carrying flags and singing traditional Simhat Torah songs.

These are special Simhat Torah flags that children wave on this day to celebrate the reading of the Torah.

Think about this
In some countries the palm and citron do not grow, so they are imported from Israel. In these countries, a single lulav and etrog may serve a whole community. A child is chosen to look after them and take them around to every family on each day of Sukkot.

HANUKKAH AND PURIM

There are two special events in history that Jews remember with festivals. Purim is the celebration of the deliverance of the Jewish people. Hanukkah, also known as the Festival of Lights, is the celebration of a victory in war. But it is also the story of a miracle. Keep reading and find out why.

Listen to a story . . .

More than 2,000 years ago, there was a Greek king in Syria. He wanted everyone in Syria to worship the Greek gods like he did. But the Jews were strong in their faith, and they refused to give up their religion. A group of Jews led by Judah the Macabee fought against the Syrians and won. When the battle was over, the Jewish soldiers went straight to the temple. They got down on their hands and knees and started to clean the temple to make it holy again. When they had finished, they went to light the lamp, but there was only enough oil for one day. They lit the lamp and celebrated until the lamp went out. But instead of one day, the lamp kept on burning and giving light for eight days. That's why today Jews celebrate Hanukkah for eight days.

On the eighth day of Hanukkah all the candles on the **menorah** [me-no-RA] are lit. Each candle represents one day of the miracle of Hanukkah.

During Hanukkah, a menorah is supposed to shine through the doorway of every Jewish home, so everyone can see the candles burning from outside.

The menorah

The menorah is the most important symbol of Hanukkah. A menorah is a candle holder that can hold a row of candles. It has always been a part of Jewish celebrations, especially the Festival of Lights. The Hanukkah menorah is different from the original menorahs in the temple. The temple menorah has seven branches to hold seven candles. The Hanukkah menorah has eight branches and a place for a ninth candle in the center. The center candle is called the *shammash* [sha-MASH], which means servant. This is because the ninth candle is used to light all the other candles.

Each letter on the dreidel is an instruction to either take out or put into the center.

Spinning the dreidel

Dreidel [DREI-dl] is a game played during Hanukkah. A dreidel is a spinning top with four sides. Each of the sides has a Hebrew letter on it. The players start by putting coins or nuts in the middle of a circle. Then they take turns spinning the top. As players spin the dreidel and a letter turns up, they take from or add to the goodies in the center. It's a fun way to pass the time while the candles in the menorah are burning.

17

Purim

Usually the synagogue is a serious place, where people go to pray and pay their respects to God. But during the festival of Purim, the atmosphere at the synagogue is very different. Purim is the celebration of a great Jewish woman's loyalty and courage in helping to save her people.

Purim *shpiels* [SHPILS] like this one are a common sight in the streets of Israel during Purim.

Listen to a story . . .

According to the Old Testament, King Ahasuerus of Persia was married to a Jewish girl named Esther. The king's chief minister, Haman, didn't like Jews, and tried to persuade the king to have them all killed. Queen Esther's cousin, Mordecai, asked Esther to convince the king to save her people. When Esther went to the king, he stopped Haman from killing the Jews by putting Haman and his followers to death instead.

Purim in the synagogue

Nobody knows whether the story of Esther is true or not, but on the day of Purim, the people of Israel celebrate. Like other celebrations, there is a service in the synagogue. But during Purim, people behave very differently than they do normally. During the Purim services, the story of Esther is read out loud. Whenever the reader comes to the name of Haman, everyone drowns out his name with noisemakers called *gregers* [GRAY-gurs]. This erases the name of the man who tried to murder the Jews and helps to make people forget him.

This boy is dressed up for Purim as Moses carrying the ten commandments.

Gifts and masquerades

Purim is a time of giving gifts to friends, family, and the poor. Looking after the poor or less fortunate is an important part of Purim. Large masquerade balls and parties are organized to help raise money for charities. At these balls, people dress up in disguises and masks, and they dance and sing throughout the night.

Often a Purim shpiel, or play, telling the story of Esther is performed with costumes and music. All of this fun is accompanied by lots of food and game-playing, making it a favorite festival for all Israelis, especially children. At Purim, the streets are filled with children wearing costumes and having fun. It is a little like Halloween, but without the jack-o-lanterns and the trick-or-treating.

Think about this

On Purim there was once a custom of choosing a Purim rabbi from among the schoolchildren of a town. This Purim rabbi would be a rabbi for one day and was allowed to make jokes about anything or anyone.

These four children must be on their way to one of the fantastic masquerades so popular at Purim.

CELEBRATING ISRAEL

Before 1948, there was no country called Israel. When the United Nations declared Israel a nation in that year, it was the first time the Jewish people had had a homeland of their own in nearly 2,000 years. The only problem was that the land given to the Jews was part of the area of the Middle East called Palestine. At that time, Palestine was under the control of the British. The British had allowed Jewish people to come from other countries and settle in Palestine since the late 1800s. But there were fights between the Arab people already living in Palestine and the new Jewish settlers. Some people, both Arabs and Jews, still fight over who the land belongs to, but most people are trying to work toward peace in the Middle East.

Immigrants arriving to the new land of Israel in 1948, the year the country was formed.

A mother mourns over the grave of her child. Memorial Day is an important reminder of the cost of independence.

Memorial Day

Not all of Israel's neighbors were happy to give up their land so that the Jews could have a country of their own. There have been a number of wars between Israel and other Middle Eastern countries. Some pieces of land are still being fought over. In the wars and battles that have been fought over the years, thousands of people have been killed. On Memorial Day, the people who died in these wars are remembered.

Memorial Day is observed the day before Independence Day to remind people what it cost to gain independence. Many people go to the cemeteries to pay their respects to the war dead. During Memorial Day, there is a two-minute period of silence to remember the dead. Television and radio stations broadcast stories and films about the famous battles that have taken place over the years. People are sad when they remember those who have suffered.

Independence Day

At sundown on the eve of Independence Day, the mood of the country begins to change as people begin celebrating independence. Families often go to the hills and light bonfires, sing songs, and tell stories until late at night. The next day, the real celebrations begin, with carnivals and parades all over the country. There is always a big fireworks display in the evening.

If you were in Israel on Independence Day, you might see children carrying plastic hammers and hitting each other on the head. As they strike each other, the children say "remember." This is to remind each other of the struggle the Jews have faced to become an independent country.

The Star of David is one of the symbols of Israel. It appears in the center of the Israeli flag.

Israel became an independent state on May 14, 1948, but Independence Day is celebrated on the fifth day of the Hebrew month of Iyar. This is because in 1948, May 14 fell on the fifth day of Iyar.

Remembering the Holocaust

During World War II, millions of Jews were killed by the Nazis. This event is called the **Holocaust**. When the Jews living in Palestine heard about the things that were happening to the Jews in Europe, they began to fast and pray for them. The fast began on December 2, 1942. The people of Israel remember this terrible time in Jewish history every December 2.

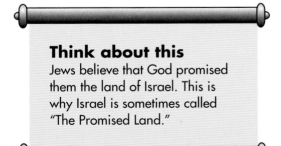

Think about this
Jews believe that God promised them the land of Israel. This is why Israel is sometimes called "The Promised Land."

NEW YEAR OF THE TREES

I srael is in a very dry part of the world. It does not have natural forests, and there is very little fresh water or rainfall. For this reason, trees, especially fruit trees, are very precious to the Israelis. Trees help to hold water in the ground and keep the soil from eroding. Tu bi-Shevat is the New Year or birthday of the trees—a time for celebrating the good things that trees bring and for planting new trees for future generations.

Before planting the trees, the children form a procession to celebrate the day.

One day of every school year is reserved for students to travel to the desert and plant saplings, or young trees.

Happy birthday

The Hebrew month of Shevat, which is around February, is the beginning of spring in Israel. This is a time of new life, as the trees begin to blossom after the winter months. On the 15th of Shevat, the birthday of the trees is celebrated. But why do the people need to know how old the trees are? In the Torah, there is a law that you must not eat the fruit of a tree in its first three years. In the tree's fourth year, the fruit is given to the priests. From the fifth year on, everyone may eat its fruit.

Think about this
Do other countries have special days that celebrate trees? How important is it to preserve the trees we already have? What would happen if there were no more trees?

Weddings and memories

It is an old custom to plant a tree on this day for each child born during the year. If the child is a boy, a cedar is planted. If the child is a girl, a cypress is planted. This way, the tree is always the same age as the child. In the past, when children grew up and got married, branches from their trees were woven together. The branches were used to hold up a canopy on their wedding day.

Today, all kinds of trees are planted on the 15th of Shevat. Many trees are planted to remember those who have died. In 1949, the people of Israel began planting a forest of trees to remember the Jews who were killed during the Holocaust. Six million Jews are believed to have been killed. Today, if you go to Israel you can see the forest of six million trees as you drive along the road into Jerusalem.

Even though it's an old tradition, some young people are still married under a *huppah* [hu-PA], a canopy held up by cedars and cypresses.

THINGS FOR YOU TO DO

One of the best ways to celebrate any Israeli festival is by singing and dancing. Many of the Jewish festivals have their own special songs and dances. But one of the most famous dances in Israel is a folk dance called the *hora* [ho-RA]. The hora is danced to any music with two beats per measure. There's a Sukkot song on the next page that's perfect for dancing the hora.

The Hora

1. Step to the left with your left foot.
2. Cross your right foot behind your left.
3. Step to the left with your left foot.
4. Hop on your left foot and swing your right foot across in front of your left foot.
5. Step in place with your right foot.
6. Hop on your right foot and swing your left foot across in front of your right foot.
7. Repeat this until the song is over.

When you've learned the steps yourself, teach some friends to dance the hora. Form a circle and join hands or hold onto each other's elbows while you count out the steps. Once you've learned the Sukkot song, you can sing along as well.

Yom Tov Lanu

Yom tov la - nu hag sa - mé - ah y' - la - dim na - gi - la na l' - su - ka - te - nu

ba o - ré - ah av - ra - ham a - vi - nu ba - ruh ha - ba ya - had ha - hag na - hog

b' - lu - lav ha - das et - rog hoy he - ah nis - mah m' - od u - va - ma - a - gal nir - kod

A holiday for us
A happy holiday children enjoy
Abraham, our father, visits our sukkah
Blessing upon him
Together we will celebrate the holiday with
lulav and etrog
We will dance in a circle.

Things to look for in your library

ABC: The Alef-Bet Book. Florence Cassen Mayers (Harry N. Abrams, 1989).
Children of Israel. Connie Buckman (Abdo & Daughters, 1994).
Count Your Way Through Israel. James Haskins (Carolrhoda Books, 1990).
Dropping in on Israel. David C. King (Rourke Publishing Group, 1995).
Jewish Holiday Songs for Children. Rachel Buchman (compact disk).
Life on an Israeli Kibbutz. Linda Jacobs Altman (Lucent Books, 1996).
Postcards from Israel. Denise Allard (Raintree/Steck Vaughn, 1997).
For a catalog of Jewish music write to: Tia's Simcha Songs, Global Village Music, 245 West
    29th St., New York, NY 10001

MAKE A MEGILLAH

A *megillah* [me-gi-LA] is a scroll. The Torah is made up of five different scrolls, or megillot. On the eve of Purim, the megillah that tells the story of Esther is read. You can make your own megillah by following these instructions.

You will need:
1. Two long cardboard tubes (from a roll of aluminum foil)
2. A long sheet of paper, or three sheets of regular paper glued together
3. Glue
4. Colored markers
5. A paintbrush
6. Watercolors
7. A colored ribbon

1 Write out the story of Esther in your own words on the paper (the story of Esther is on page 18). Use the paints or markers to illustrate your story.

2 Decorate the ends of the cardboard tubes with colorful patterns. You might like to use the star that appears on the Israeli flag, called the Star of David.

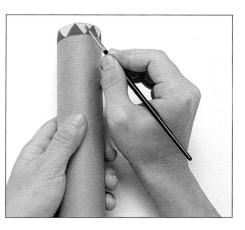

3 Glue each end of the paper to one of the cardboard tubes.

4 When the glue has dried, roll the paper onto the tubes.

5 Tie the scroll with the ribbon. Now you are ready to read your own megillah to your friends on Purim.

The Story of Esther

Many years ago King Ahasuerus married a Jewish girl named Esther. The King's minister didn't like Jews. He wanted to kill them all. But Esther convinced the King to save the Jews.

MAKE HAMANTASHEN

A favorite food served during Purim is *hamantashen* [ha-MAN-ta-shn]. These are sweet cakes or cookies, sometimes made with prunes or chocolate chips. Hamantashen means "Haman's ears." They're named after the man in the Book of Esther in the Bible who tried to have the Jews killed.

You will need:
1. ½ cup (70 g) sifted flour
2. 2 teaspoons baking powder
3. ⅝ cup (125 g) sugar
4. ⅝ cup (125 g) butter
5. ¾ cup (150 g) chocolate chips
6. 2 eggs
7. 1 teaspoon vanilla
8. A wooden spoon
9. A spatula
10. A baking tray
11. A potholder
12. Measuring cups
13. Measuring spoons

1 Mix the flour and baking powder together in a bowl.

2 Cut in the butter until the mixture is smooth.

3 Beat the eggs and add them and the vanilla to the flour mixture.

4 When the mixture is smooth, drop a small amount onto the greased tray and top with a few chocolate chips. Keep on doing this until you've used all the mixture—about 24 cookies.

5 Bake the cookies in a moderate oven, 350°F (180°C) for 15–20 minutes. Be careful with the hot oven—be sure to use the potholder or have an adult help you take the cookies out.

GLOSSARY

etrog, 14 — A type of citrus fruit called a citron in English. It is carried during the harvest festival Sukkot.

gregers, 18 — Noisemakers used during Purim to drown out the name of Haman.

Haggadah, 8 — The story read at the dinner table during Pesach.

hametz, 10 — Leaven. The ingredient in bread that makes it rise.

Holocaust, 23 — The death of millions of Jews during World War II at the hands of the Nazis.

lulav, 14 — Branches from palm, willow, and myrtle trees.

matzah, 9 — A type of bread made without yeast and eaten during Pesach.

menorah, 16 — A seven- or eight-branched candle holder. The Hanukkah menorah has nine branches.

minority, 5 — A group of people within a larger group.

Seder, 8 — The special meal laid out at Pesach.

sukkah, 12 — Huts that the Hebrews lived in after they escaped from Egypt.

Torah, 4 — The Jewish holy book.

INDEX